DINOSAUR
REVEALED

Written by
DOUGAL DIXON

LONDON, NEW YORK, MUNICH,
MELBOURNE, and DELHI

SENIOR EDITOR SIMON HOLLAND
EDITOR CHARLOTTE HURDMAN
DESIGNERS JIM GREEN, JOANNE LITTLE,
AND ADRIENNE HUTCHINSON
3-D ILLUSTRATOR MARK LONGWORTH
MANAGING EDITOR CAMILLA HALLINAN
MANAGING ART EDITOR SOPHIA TAMPAKOPOULOS
CATEGORY PUBLISHER SUE GRABHAM
ART DIRECTOR MARK RICHARDS
PICTURE RESEARCHER BRIDGET TILLY
JACKET DESIGNER BOB WARNER
DTP DESIGNER ERIC SHAPLAND
PRODUCTION CONTROLLER DULCIE ROWE

First published in Great Britain in 2003
by Dorling Kindersley Limited,
80 Strand, London WC2R 0RL

2 4 6 8 10 9 7 5 3 1

A CIP catalogue record for this book
is available from the British Library.

ISBN 0-7513-6821-0

Colour reproduction by
Colourscan, Singapore
Printed in China by
Leo Paper Products

Discover more at
www.dk.com

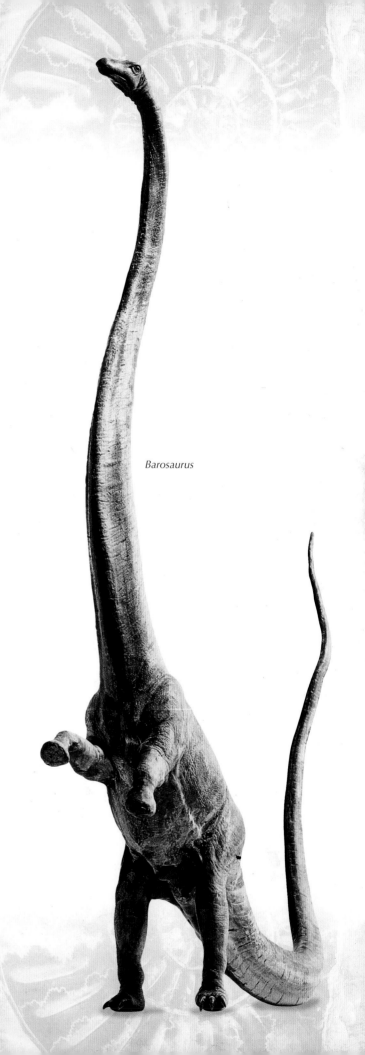

Barosaurus

CONTENTS

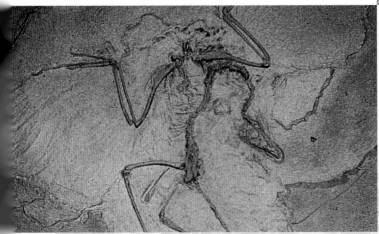

A PREHISTORIC WORLD

THE WORLD OF THE DINOSAURS is a mysterious place to us. It is rooted millions and millions of years into the past. We can never experience it directly – only through the fossils that we find, the structure of rocks and material in the earth, and the scientific studies that give us an idea of what the world was like at that time. Some of this evidence is reliable, but much of it needs to be pieced together by experts, who argue over and discuss the things we do not know for certain. We know what animals and plants lived during the different periods of the Mesozoic Era (the age of the dinosaurs), but their relationships and individual lifestyles are not so clear. This is why palaeontology – the study of fossils – is so exciting. We will never know absolutely everything about the dinosaur age, but each new scrap of information makes our vision of this prehistoric world a little clearer.

A working, radio-controlled model Pteranodon *– a typical pterosaur*

IN THE AIR

The most common flying animals of the Mesozoic Era were distant relatives of the dinosaurs, known as pterosaurs. A typical pterosaur was covered in fur, had light, hollow bones, and flew on thin, membranous wings. The wings were attached to the sides of the body, and supported by a fourth finger as thick as its arm.

Iguana – a typical lizard

Sculptors and artists use modern animals, such as lizards, as a guide to the colour and texture of dinosaur skin

"TERRIBLE LIZARDS"

The word dinosaur means "terrible lizard". This name was invented by the 19th-century scientists who first studied the dinosaurs, and who immediately noticed their lizard-like bone structure and teeth. Although true lizards such as the iguana did exist alongside dinosaurs such as *Psittacosaurus*, the two were from very different groups of animals.

Corythosaurus **skin texture**, *preserved in mud*

Psittacosaurus *was a typical ornithopod – a two-legged, plant-eating dinosaur*

SKIN IMPRESSIONS

Fossils can be formed when part of a plant or animal wastes away but leaves behind an impression of itself. The skin of a dinosaur does not fossilize very easily – but sometimes, if the dinosaur were encased in mud shortly after death, the mud would take an impression of its skin texture. This skin impression of a duck-billed *Corythosaurus* tells us that the dinosaur's skin was made up of a tight "mosaic" pattern of rounded, non-overlapping scales.

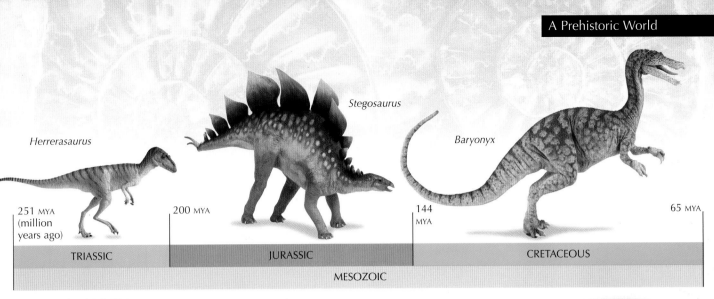

Herrerasaurus

Stegosaurus

Baryonyx

| 251 MYA (million years ago) | 200 MYA | 144 MYA | 65 MYA |
| TRIASSIC | JURASSIC | CRETACEOUS |
| MESOZOIC |

THE MESOZOIC ERA

The age of the dinosaurs lasted some 160 million years, from late in the Triassic period to the end of the Cretaceous. During this immense period of time, the dinosaurs evolved from small, lizard-like animals to some of the biggest animals the world has ever seen. Triassic *Herrerasaurus* was an early species of dinosaur that would have developed into the main lines of the ornithischian (bird-hipped), plant-eating dinosaurs such as *Stegosaurus* and the saurischian (lizard-hipped) dinosaurs such as *Baryonyx*.

Elasmosaurus was typical of the long-necked, fish-eating plesiosaurs

INNER WORKINGS

The sauropods were huge, four-legged, plant-eating dinosaurs. Their enormous size raises all sorts of questions about their lifestyle and bodily workings. For example, if *Brachiosaurus* was a warm-blooded animal – able to keep its body temperature at a constant level, as a human being does – it would have needed vast amounts of food to keep its massive body going. In its natural environment, there might not have been enough food around for the dinosaur to feed itself in this way. So, while some dinosaurs may have been warm-blooded, the sauropods were probably not.

A size comparison between Brachiosaurus – one of the largest land animals of all time – and a human being

IN THE OCEAN

There were lots of marine animals during dinosaur times. As well as strange fish and invertebrates (creatures without a backbone), there were long-necked plesiosaurs, fish-shaped ichthyosaurs, and swimming, lizard-like mosasaurs. These three groups of creatures all preyed on fish, and one another, in the Mesozoic seas – but none of these swimming reptiles was related to the dinosaurs.

Brachiosaurus – a large sauropod dinosaur

NEW LIFE

O N A SMALL ISLAND off the shore of a shallow lake, a group of *Troodon*s formed a nesting colony in an area now known as Egg Mountain in Montana, USA. The female *Troodon*s dug wide, shallow pits in the earth and laid two eggs at a time – moving around the nest until they had produced a clutch of up to 24 eggs. Inside each egg, a foetus (baby) grew until its coiled form filled the egg to bursting point. When ready to hatch, the baby uncoiled itself – splitting off the top part of the egg.

A FOSSILIZED *TROODON* EGG
Only the bottom two-thirds of this fossilized *Troodon* egg, where it was buried in the mud, have been preserved. This is enough information, however, to reconstruct the whole egg and foetus. A complete *Troodon* egg would have been about 15 cm (6 in) in length.

The impression of the left leg bones and part of the jaw allow us to identify the whole baby animal

The thin eggshell has been replaced by minerals that preserve the nature of the egg's construction

NEST CONSTRUCTION
In a *Troodon* nest, each egg was embedded in the mud to keep it warm, with only its top third exposed to the air. *Troodon* parents protected their eggs from the weather by covering the nest with a layer of foliage. The nests in the colony were about 2 m (6 ft) wide and were spaced about 2 m (6 ft) apart from one another, so that each nest was beyond the reach of neighbouring adults.

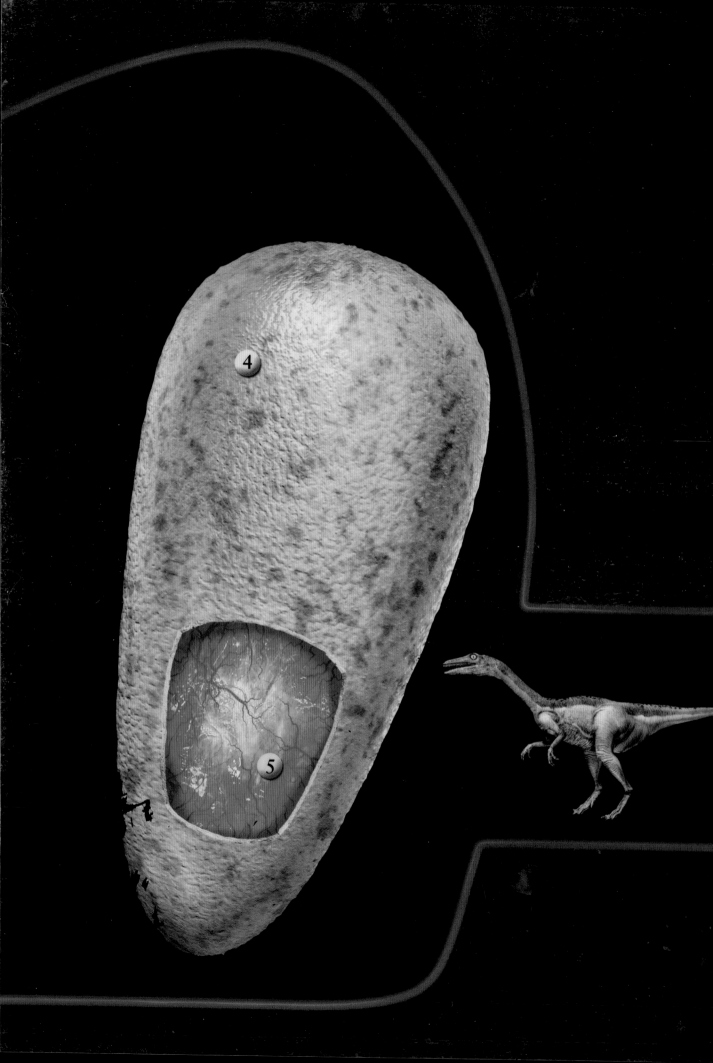

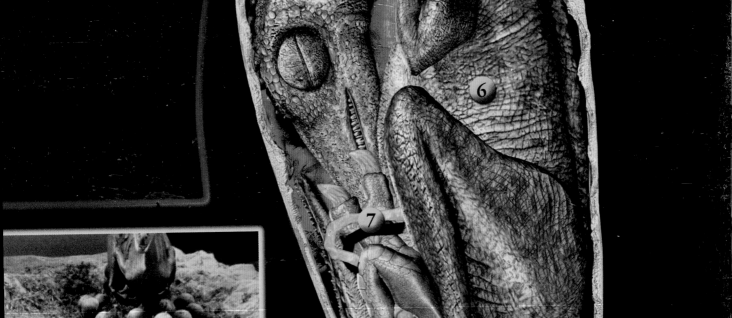

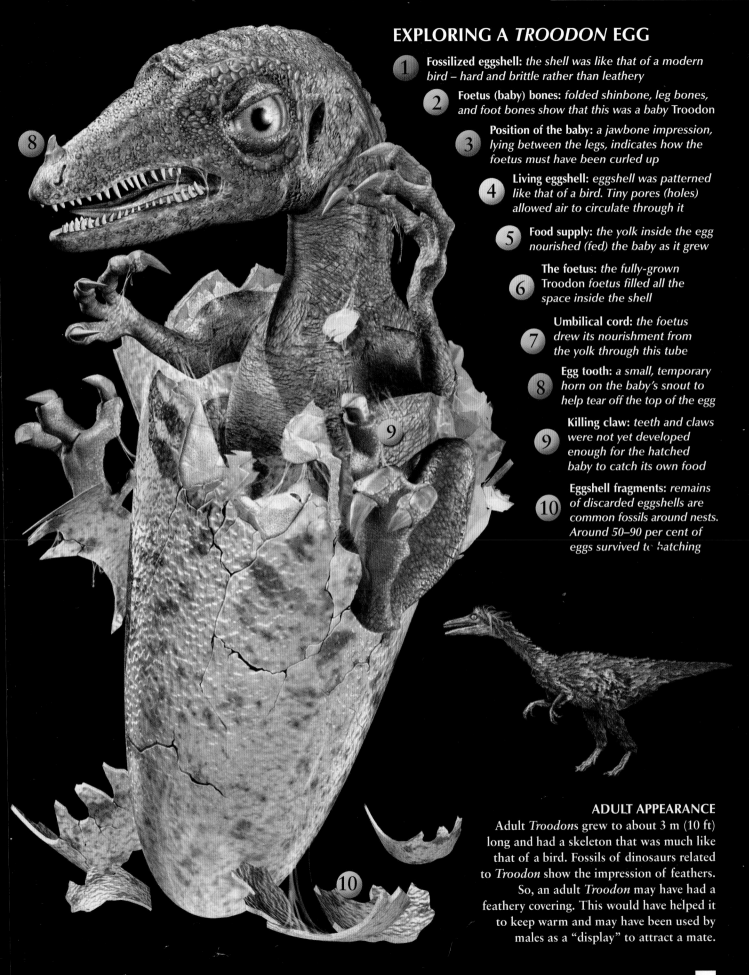

EXPLORING A *TROODON* EGG

1 **Fossilized eggshell:** *the shell was like that of a modern bird – hard and brittle rather than leathery*

2 **Foetus (baby) bones:** *folded shinbone, leg bones, and foot bones show that this was a baby* Troodon

3 **Position of the baby:** *a jawbone impression, lying between the legs, indicates how the foetus must have been curled up*

4 **Living eggshell:** *eggshell was patterned like that of a bird. Tiny pores (holes) allowed air to circulate through it*

5 **Food supply:** *the yolk inside the egg nourished (fed) the baby as it grew*

6 **The foetus:** *the fully-grown* Troodon *foetus filled all the space inside the shell*

7 **Umbilical cord:** *the foetus drew its nourishment from the yolk through this tube*

8 **Egg tooth:** *a small, temporary horn on the baby's snout to help tear off the top of the egg*

9 **Killing claw:** *teeth and claws were not yet developed enough for the hatched baby to catch its own food*

10 **Eggshell fragments:** *remains of discarded eggshells are common fossils around nests. Around 50–90 per cent of eggs survived to hatching*

ADULT APPEARANCE

Adult *Troodon*s grew to about 3 m (10 ft) long and had a skeleton that was much like that of a bird. Fossils of dinosaurs related to *Troodon* show the impression of feathers. So, an adult *Troodon* may have had a feathery covering. This would have helped it to keep warm and may have been used by males as a "display" to attract a mate.

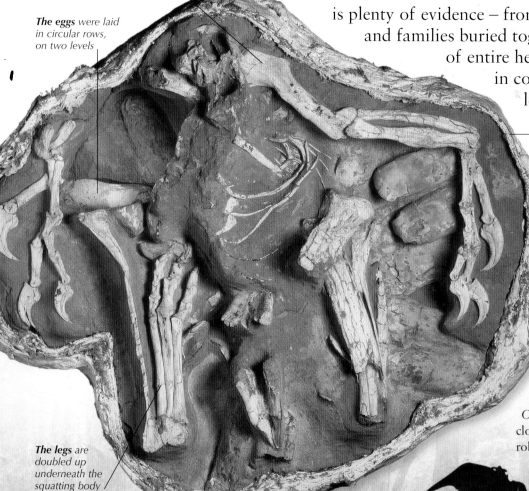

Egg fossils in their nest

FRAGILE EVIDENCE
The nests discovered in the Gobi Desert contained circle-shaped rows of eggs, laid in a shallow pit scooped out of sand. Each egg was about the size of a slipper.

EXPEDITIONS TO THE GOBI
In the 1920s, an expedition from the American Museum of Natural History, led by Roy Chapman Andrews (above, right), discovered dinosaur nesting sites in the Gobi Desert of Mongolia. These were the first recognizable dinosaur nests to be found. This discovery proved what experts had always thought – that dinosaurs laid their eggs in nests.

Oviraptor spread out its arms so that its wing feathers (not preserved) covered and protected the eggs

The eggs were laid in circular rows, on two levels

The legs are doubled up underneath the squatting body

FAMILY GROUPS

THE IMAGE OF THE DINOSAUR as a lone hunter, aggressively challenging anything that crossed its path, is largely wrong. As is the idea of the dinosaur as a massive beast, chewing its way through ancient forests with a cold, reptilian disregard for any other living thing. In fact, many dinosaurs seem to have been very sociable animals. There is plenty of evidence – from fossilized nesting sites and families buried together, to the preservation of entire herds – that dinosaurs lived in complex social groups and led tightly-knit family lives.

This plaster rim around the specimen is roughly the same size and shape as the nest

A CARING PARENT
In 1993, an expedition to the Gobi Desert found the skeleton of an *Oviraptor* brooding (looking after) the eggs in its nest. The adult may have been protecting the young from a sandstorm or flood at the moment of its death. For 70 years, scientists had thought that the eggs in the Gobi belonged to a frilled dinosaur called *Protoceratops*. They also believed that a meat-eating *Oviraptor*, whose bones were found close by, was killed while robbing a nest.

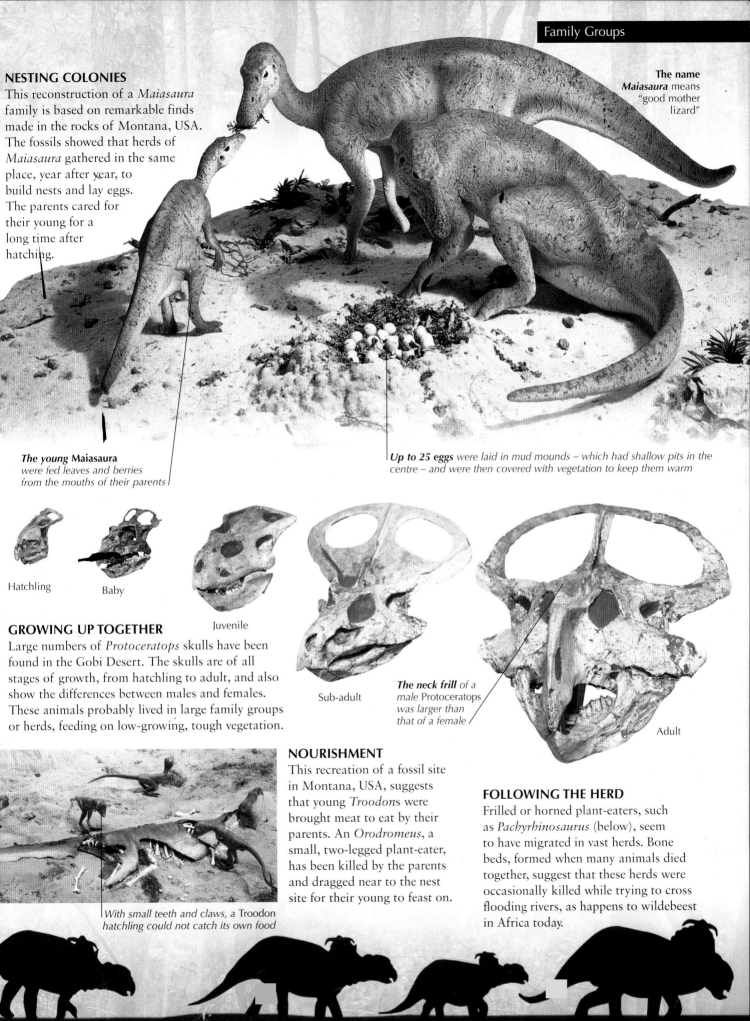

NESTING COLONIES

This reconstruction of a *Maiasaura* family is based on remarkable finds made in the rocks of Montana, USA. The fossils showed that herds of *Maiasaura* gathered in the same place, year after year, to build nests and lay eggs. The parents cared for their young for a long time after hatching.

The name *Maiasaura* means "good mother lizard"

The young Maiasaura were fed leaves and berries from the mouths of their parents

Up to 25 eggs were laid in mud mounds – which had shallow pits in the centre – and were then covered with vegetation to keep them warm

Hatchling

Baby

Juvenile

Sub-adult

The neck frill of a male Protoceratops was larger than that of a female

Adult

GROWING UP TOGETHER

Large numbers of *Protoceratops* skulls have been found in the Gobi Desert. The skulls are of all stages of growth, from hatchling to adult, and also show the differences between males and females. These animals probably lived in large family groups or herds, feeding on low-growing, tough vegetation.

NOURISHMENT

This recreation of a fossil site in Montana, USA, suggests that young *Troodon*s were brought meat to eat by their parents. An *Orodromeus*, a small, two-legged plant-eater, has been killed by the parents and dragged near to the nest site for their young to feast on.

With small teeth and claws, a Troodon hatchling could not catch its own food

FOLLOWING THE HERD

Frilled or horned plant-eaters, such as *Pachyrhinosaurus* (below), seem to have migrated in vast herds. Bone beds, formed when many animals died together, suggest that these herds were occasionally killed while trying to cross flooding rivers, as happens to wildebeest in Africa today.

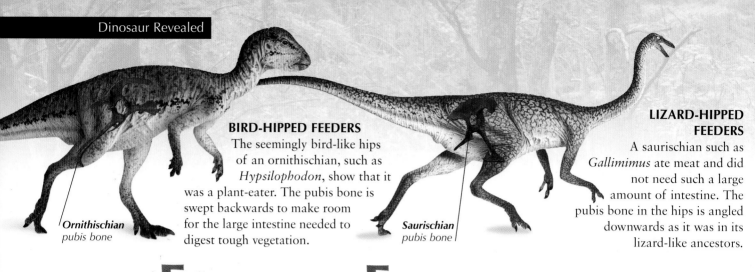

BIRD-HIPPED FEEDERS
The seemingly bird-like hips of an ornithischian, such as *Hypsilophodon*, show that it was a plant-eater. The pubis bone is swept backwards to make room for the large intestine needed to digest tough vegetation.

Ornithischian pubis bone

Saurischian pubis bone

LIZARD-HIPPED FEEDERS
A saurischian such as *Gallimimus* ate meat and did not need such a large amount of intestine. The pubis bone in the hips is angled downwards as it was in its lizard-like ancestors.

FEEDING FEATURES

YOU CAN TELL MANY THINGS by looking at an animal's teeth, such as its age, but most importantly you can tell what it eats. Different-shaped teeth are needed to eat different foods. Teeth are made of a very hard substance and fossilize easily. This is why they are so useful to the study of dinosaurs. Other aspects of a dinosaur's anatomy also give us clues to its diet. The shape and arrangement of the jaws are revealing, as are the hip bones. Dinosaurs are split into two groups: ornithischian (bird-hipped) dinosaurs were all plant-eaters, but the saurischian (lizard-hipped) group contained both plant- and meat-eaters.

Albertosaurus had sharp, curved teeth that re-grew if they fell out during a fight

INSIDE THE MOUTH OF A CARNIVORE
The skull of *Albertosaurus* shows the typical layout of a big meat-eating dinosaur's mouth. The very long jaws formed a huge gape, so that the dinosaur could swallow huge chunks of flesh. The teeth were saw-edged for shearing meat off the bone. Those at the front were stronger in order to hold on to struggling prey.

THE JAWS OF A FISH-EATER
A few dinosaurs, such as *Suchomimus* and its relatives, ate fish. This is proved by fish bones and scales that have been found in their stomachs. Their long and narrow jaws were slim and streamlined for slicing through water, while lots of small, pointed teeth gripped on to the slippery prey.

The jaws of Suchomimus were like those of a fish-eating crocodile

*A **Velociraptor attack*** *from all sides caused a lot of distraction and confusion for the prey*

*A **long, stiff tail*** *acted as a good counter-balance when pursuing prey*

PACK ATTACKS

It is likely that many of the small meat-eating dinosaurs hunted in packs to bring down larger prey more efficiently. The swift-running *Velociraptor* belonged to a group known as the maniraptoran ("grasping hand") dinosaurs. Evidence of their group attacks shows that these creatures were among the most intelligent of the dinosaurs, although they were only as clever as some of today's dumbest birds. They probably worked together to bring down bigger animals such as *Protoceratops*.

The longer claw *on the second toe could slash through the flesh of Velociraptor's prey*

Protoceratops's beak *could inflict damage on an attacker in front. But its only protection was a slim neck shield*

LONE SCAVENGERS

Meat-eating dinosaurs may not always have killed their own prey. Although we know that tiny *Compsognathus* was agile enough to catch and eat lizards, it may also have scavenged from the corpses of dead animals. This may also be true of the really large meat-eaters like *Tyrannosaurus*. It is difficult to tell, from fossil remains, which was the more common lifestyle.

Compsognathus

CHEWERS

Ornithopods such as *Corythosaurus*, a duck-billed dinosaur, had row upon row of grating and grinding cheek teeth for mashing plant material to a pulp before swallowing it. They may also have had cheek pouches to hold the food while they were chewing. This meant that they could process a large amount of food at once.

Cheek teeth

Corythosaurus *used its narrow bill to pick out food to be chewed*

Most meat-eaters *had small arms*

SWALLOWERS

Sauropods such as *Diplodocus* did not have time to chew their food – they just raked it in and swallowed it continuously to feed their huge bulk. They probably swallowed stones, as well, to help grind up the food in their stomachs. These stomach stones are called gastroliths.

The peg-like teeth of Diplodocus *were used to rake leaves from branches*

THE MESOZOIC EARTH

During the Mesozoic Era the Earth's landmasses changed. The Triassic was the time of Pangaea, the supercontinent that included all the land regions of the Earth. Pangaea began to break up and drift apart in the Jurassic, and by the end of Cretaceous times the continents had broken up into land outlines that slowly began to resemble the islands and continents of today.

Triassic period
c. 251–200 MYA – a single landmass

Jurassic period
c. 200–144 MYA – Pangaea landmass begins to split up

Cretaceous period
c. 144–65 MYA – modern continents start to appear

THROUGH THE AGES

THE EARTH HAS BEEN IN EXISTENCE for about 4,600 million years. Life of one kind or another has existed on Earth for most of that time – ever since conditions were cool enough to allow it. The dinosaurs existed for only 170 million years of this immense period, which is about 100 times as long as humans have been around. During this period of 170 million years, the face of the Earth changed dramatically. Continents moved, climates changed, and vegetation evolved. In fact, the earliest dinosaurs, of the Triassic, would have had trouble surviving the very different environmental conditions experienced by the last dinosaurs of the Cretaceous.

Ginkgo

PLANT IMPRINTS

A 160-million-year-old fossil imprint of ginkgo leaves shows that the plant was almost identical to how it is today. The Mesozoic was a time of radical change, but some plants have altered very little.

THE TRIASSIC WORLD

When the dinosaurs first appeared, the Pangaean continent was full of deserts, with widespread vegetation only around the coastlines. Many other animals evolved along with the dinosaurs at this time, including the flying pterosaurs and the early relatives of mammals.

Fern leaves

TRIASSIC FOLIAGE

In regions near water, ferns, tree ferns, and horsetails thrived – as did forests of primitive conifers, such as monkey-puzzle trees.

Eudimorphon *was one of the first pterosaurs to flap through the air during the Triassic period*

JURASSIC FOLIAGE

The spreading, shallow seas and new oceans of the Jurassic filled the rifts (gaps) between continents. This meant that wet climates and lush vegetation became more common. Jurassic forests were full of conifers – most of them similar to the primitive types of the Triassic – as well as cycads and cycad-like plants. The undergrowth was now home to a varied range of ferns and horsetails.

Cycad leaves

Barosaurus – a sauropod dinosaur

Horsetail

JURASSIC WORLD

The Jurassic was a time when the Earth's environments were kinder to dinosaurs. Forests of cycad, conifer, and sequoia trees flourished in warm, wet climates. These lush conditions gave rise to new kinds of giant, plant-eating sauropod dinosaurs, such as *Apatosaurus*, *Diplodocus*, and *Brachiosaurus* – the largest animals ever to walk on the Earth.

Passion flower

Magnolia

FLOWERING PLANTS

The late Cretaceous saw the development of flowering plants. Broad-leaved trees, such as dogwood and magnolia, began to occupy forests along with the older, conifer species such as pines and yews. Flowering herbs were also spreading through the undergrowth. There was still no grass, however. Grasses did not appear until after the era of dinosaurs.

CRETACEOUS WORLD

In Cretaceous times, the continents were broken up. Different groups of dinosaurs developed on different landmasses, separated from one another. Despite their later extinction, this was the peak time of dinosaur development. The horned ceratopsians, such as *Pentaceratops*, were among the last to evolve.

Pentaceratops

TYRANNOSAURUS RETURNS

A FEROCIOUS-LOOKING *TYRANNOSAURUS* STRUTS the dark halls of a natural history museum. A reconstruction of its skeleton provides the framework for scientists and artists to build up a complete picture of what *Tyrannosaurus* was like in real life. From mineralized bones, and other fossil evidence, its flesh, internal organs, and skin can all be restored, using computer-generated graphics, to show us what this beast might have looked like as a living, breathing creature.

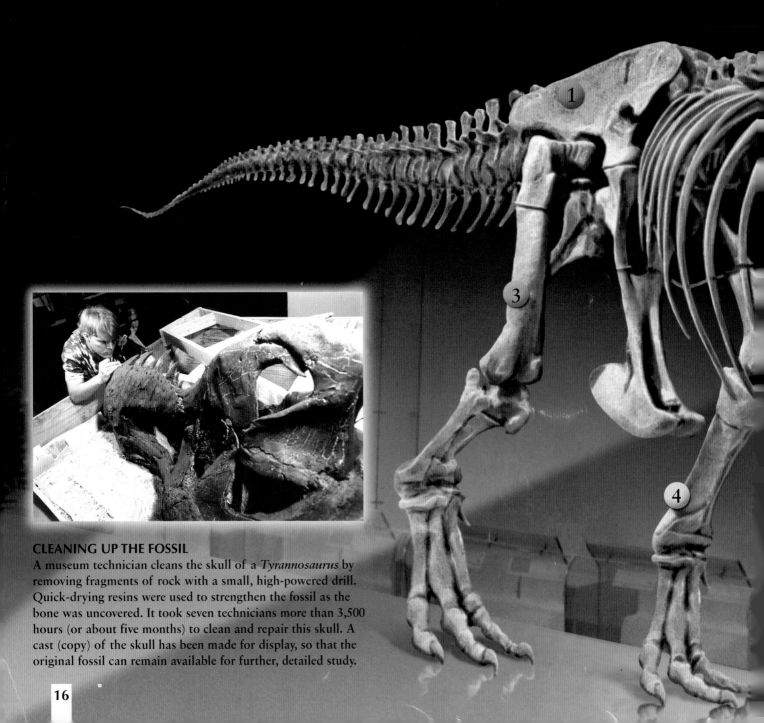

CLEANING UP THE FOSSIL

A museum technician cleans the skull of a *Tyrannosaurus* by removing fragments of rock with a small, high-powered drill. Quick-drying resins were used to strengthen the fossil as the bone was uncovered. It took seven technicians more than 3,500 hours (or about five months) to clean and repair this skull. A cast (copy) of the skull has been made for display, so that the original fossil can remain available for further, detailed study.

EXPLORING A *TYRANNOSAURUS* RESTORATION

1 **Skeleton:** *usually, lightweight casts of the original fossil bones are used in a reconstruction of the skeleton*

2 **Missing bones:** *sometimes, it is necessary to model bones using a best guess of what they looked like*

3 **Borrowed bones:** *skeletons are rarely found complete, so parts are borrowed from others of the same species*

4 **Muscle position:** *marks on the bones show where the muscles were attached. Scientists use these to estimate the shape and bulk of Tyrannosaurus's body*

5 **Surface mesh:** *to make the Tyrannosaurus's body contours, a 3-D grid is created on a computer*

6 **Texture:** *skin texture is added to the mesh based on fossil impressions and comparisons with living animals*

7 **Movement:** *model-makers add stretches and wrinkles to the skin to show how the animal moved its body*

8 **Colour and detail:** *the realistic colour tones are based on those of modern animals that share a similar lifestyle. Claws, horns, teeth, and eyes are also added*

FINDING AND DATING THE SITE

Dinosaur hunters need to know the age of the rocks they are working on. They can often tell this from fossils that are far more common than dinosaur fossils. Certain fossil animals, such as these ammonites, existed for only a short period of time – and so their presence in a rock can be used to date that rock fairly precisely.

Ammonites are often used as index fossils – specimens that can help to date neighbouring rocks and fossils

RAISING THE DEAD

FINDING AND EXTRACTING DINOSAUR REMAINS from rocks in the ground involves all kinds of specialist techniques. First, the palaeontologists at the dig site need to know that they are looking among rocks of the right age. Each geological period has its own selection of fossils, and some of these fossils – known as "index fossils" – are so common, wide-ranging, and rapidly-evolving that when they are found they can be used to give a date to the rock itself. Dinosaurs were land-living animals, so most dinosaur excavations are done in sedimentary rocks that were laid down in deserts, swamps, rivers, or lakes – rather than in the more common sedimentary rocks that were formed under the sea.

Laquer or varnish is applied to an exposed fossil to prevent it from breaking up

Heavy hammer

Chisels

Tools of a field palaeontologist

Brushes

HOMING IN

Often, an important dinosaur site is found by accident – when a single bone is spotted at the surface of the rock, where it has been eroded (worn down by natural conditions). This may point to the presence of a complete skeleton, or it may just be an isolated fragment. Palaeontologists use various tools and brushes to make a quick investigation, and then decide whether or not to explore the site further.

The crumbling rock surface is cleared away to expose the specimen more fully

TOOLS FOR THE JOB

A palaeontologist's tools look a bit like those of a stonecutter combined with the instruments of a dentist. Field workers use heavy hammers and chisels, and even power drills, to clear away the bulk rock – known as overburden – that may cover the fossil being excavated. They also need very fine probes and brushes to expose and stabilize (protect) some of the more delicate fossil structures.

PROTECTING A MAJOR FIND

It can be difficult to move a large fossil. To protect and keep it together, palaeontologists stabilize the fossil by covering it with a jacket of plaster and bandages, replacing the original rocky covering that preserved it for millions of years. The sturdy jacket can then be transported to the laboratory in one piece.

Elmer Riggs and Robert Thorne (right) dug up the skeleton of a South American *Mastodon* on the banks of the Rio Quequen River, Argentina, in about 1910

A full skeleton is so rare that it must be treated with extreme care

A jacketed fossil can weigh many tonnes

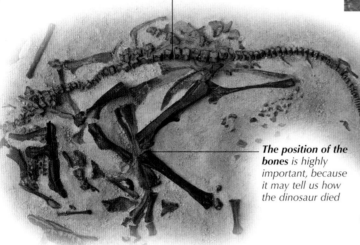

The position of the bones is highly important, because it may tell us how the dinosaur died

TRANSPORTING THE FOSSILS

A well-preserved and articulated (jointed) dinosaur skeleton – such as this hadrosaur – must be moved to the laboratory as one complete item. Once the field workers have exposed the whole skeleton, they apply a jacket to the upper surface. They then cut away the rocks beneath and turn the skeleton over. The rest of the stabilizing jacket is then applied to the fossil surfaces on the underside.

MAPPING THE FOSSIL SITE

A palaeontological team must study the entire area of the excavation site. Field workers do this by using a large grid frame to plot the position of every discovery, which is then recorded on a grid map of the site. This helps them to show how an animal came to be where it was at the time of its death. Samples of the surrounding rocks are taken away for analysis, to find out more about the environment in which the animal was preserved.

A palaeontological team may be on site for months

Micropalaeontolgists look for very tiny fossils

Grids help to map the layout of the site, and the location of the finds made there. All areas of the site are drawn and photographed

PREPARATION

In the controlled environment of the laboratory, the jacket – used to stabilize specimens at the excavation site – is carefully opened to reveal the priceless fossil. Once the plaster and bandage covering is removed, the fossil bones are cleaned using fine picks, brushes, and high-pressure air jets. The fossil technicians work very hard to clean the specimen as well as possible without damaging it.

Sequences of CAT-scan images allow technicians to study both the inside and the outside of the fossil

IN THE LAB

T HE BREATH-TAKING DISPLAY of a mounted skeleton in a museum might appear to be the end result of a dinosaur excavation – but arousing the public's interest in this way is only one of a whole set of aims that the palaeontological team is trying to achieve. Usually, a dinosaur mount is made from casts (copies) of the bones, while the precious originals are kept aside for laboratory study. Fossil workers painstakingly prepare and preserve the original bones, so that later generations of palaeontologists can also study them. Scientists also study excavated rocks from the site, to produce a more detailed picture of the animal, its habitat, and its lifestyle.

The surface detail of a Tyrannosaurus skull fossil, as revealed by CAT-scan imaging

INSIDE GUIDES

CAT-scanning is one of the modern techniques used for studying dinosaur remains. Technicians pass the specimen through a device that produces an image as a series of X-ray "slices". These slices are then put together to produce a highly-detailed, 3-D picture of the specimen, inside and out. This kind of picture can provide details of otherwise hidden aspects – such as the brain case and the nasal cavities. These things are not usually available for study while looking at the fossil only from the outside.

This skeleton was built from casts taken from the original, fossilized skeleton

The position of Stegosaurus's plates is still not fully understood

MUSEUM PIECES

A complete dinosaur skeleton, on display, is a very dramatic sight – but it may not be all that it seems. Nowadays, the original fossil bones are rarely mounted. Casts of the bones are usually made out of a robust and lightweight material like glass fibre. If some of the bones are missing, the same type may be borrowed from other skeletons or sculpted by specialist model-makers.

Some guesswork and interpretation goes into the assembly of the bone casts in a dinosaur reconstruction, based on studies of both the fossils and today's living creatures

FINISHING TOOLS

It is the job of specialist technicians, called preparators, to make a fossil bone ready for study. They use all kinds of tools and techniques to get the specimen into a better condition, so that the palaeontologist can examine it properly. For example, they remove the specimen from its matrix – the rock in which it is embedded – and stabilize it, using special protective resins, to stop it from decaying.

Glass fibre cast   **Rubber** mould

Tools used to remove a fossil from its matrix

CREATING A CAST

As part of their work, preparators make replica casts of bones. First, they create a mould for the cast using liquid synthetic rubber, which they press against the surfaces of the fossil itself. This produces a negative form (impression) of the original, which is then filled in with a solidifying, modelling material such as glass fibre. Once this has set, the mould is cut open to reveal a cast that is identical, in form and texture, to the original fossil.

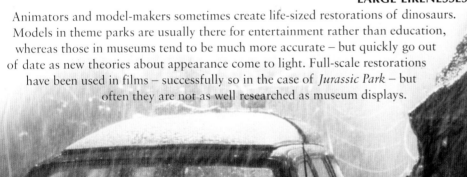

In an anatomical model, the bones may be the only elements directly based on fossil evidence

The position of internal organs is suggested by the shape of the body, or by comparison with modern animals

Skin texture is sometimes known from imprints left in fossilized mud

3-D, anatomical restoration of *Carnotaurus*

3-D THEORIES

A mounted skeleton in a museum is known as a reconstruction. When all the information about a specimen is put together, it may also be possible to build up a more complete picture of the animal. A model or sculpture of a fossil animal, as it may have looked when it was alive, is known as a restoration.

LARGE LIKENESSES

Animators and model-makers sometimes create life-sized restorations of dinosaurs. Models in theme parks are usually there for entertainment rather than education, whereas those in museums tend to be much more accurate – but quickly go out of date as new theories about appearance come to light. Full-scale restorations have been used in films – successfully so in the case of *Jurassic Park* – but often they are not as well researched as museum displays.

THE BONE WARS

The greatest advances in dinosaur knowledge during the 19th century were made by two rival scientists – Othniel Charles Marsh (far left) and Edward Drinker Cope (left). These men were great rivals, and their teams fiercely competed against each other for new finds across the wild North American frontier. Thanks to this intense rivalry, 130 new species were known by the time these "bone wars" stopped at the end of the 1890s.

Meat-eating teeth

HISTORY OF DISCOVERY

IT IS AN ADVENTURE, DISCOVERING NEW dinosaurs. Every bit of information we find adds to our knowledge of what things were like long ago. New discoveries are being made all the time, so the study of palaeontology never stands still. In the early days of dinosaur hunting, more than a century-and-a-half ago, scientists went out into unknown places and suffered the hardships of disease, hunger, and isolation – just like all early explorers. Today, with satellite communication and other forms of technical back-up, things are not quite so difficult – but modern discoveries are every bit as exciting. There is still a great deal to learn and each new specimen may radically alter our thinking.

Megalosaurus's jaws and teeth were very much like those of a huge lizard

FIRST FINDS

The first dinosaur fossil to be described and named was the lower jaw and teeth of *Megalosaurus*. It was recorded by William Buckland of Oxford, England, in 1824. Prior to this, in the 18th century, many fossilized dinosaur bones had been found in England, but they had not been scientifically studied and identified.

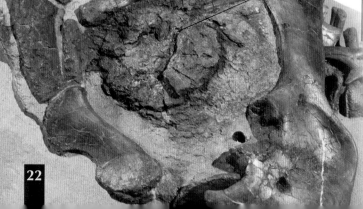

The rib cage was preserved in three dimensions, and was not flattened

The heart

Thescelosaurus was a swift-footed, plant-eating ornithopod dinosaur

ORGAN PRINTS

Usually, only the hard parts of a dinosaur – the bones and the teeth – are preserved as fossils. We are very rarely lucky enough to find the remains of the softer organs. In 2000, the skeleton of the ornithopod *Thescelosaurus* was found in South Dakota, USA, with a lump in its chest that experts believe to be the fossilized heart. In other finds, the liver, intestines, and some of the muscles have been preserved.

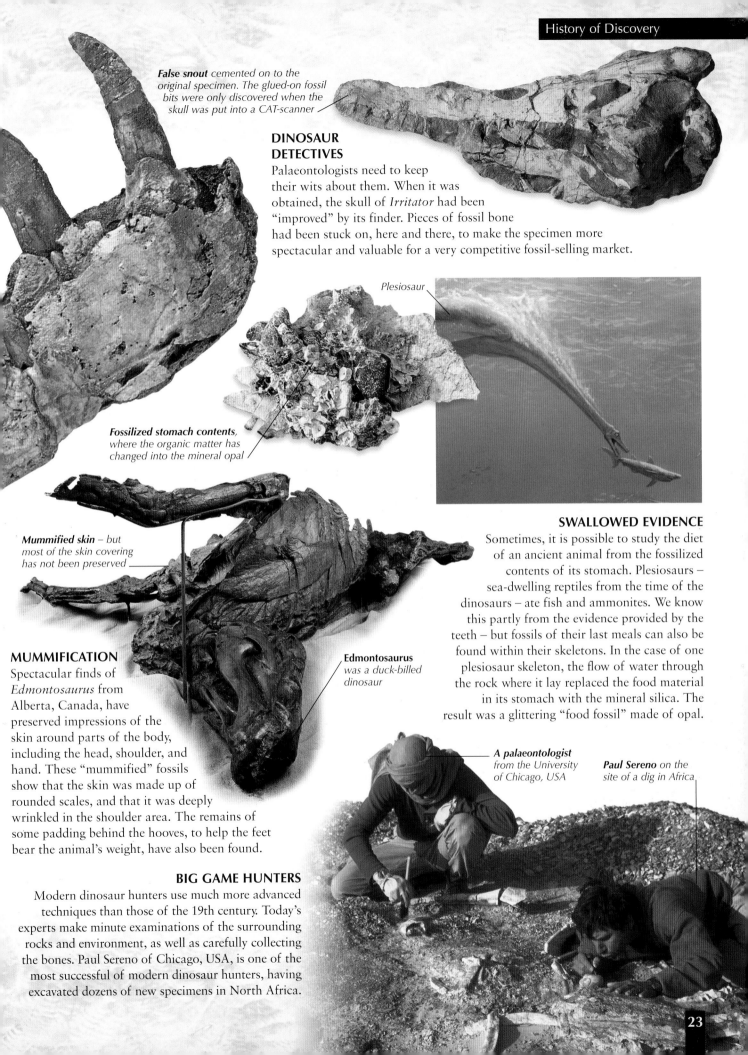

False snout cemented on to the original specimen. The glued-on fossil bits were only discovered when the skull was put into a CAT-scanner

DINOSAUR DETECTIVES

Palaeontologists need to keep their wits about them. When it was obtained, the skull of *Irritator* had been "improved" by its finder. Pieces of fossil bone had been stuck on, here and there, to make the specimen more spectacular and valuable for a very competitive fossil-selling market.

Plesiosaur

Fossilized stomach contents, where the organic matter has changed into the mineral opal

SWALLOWED EVIDENCE

Sometimes, it is possible to study the diet of an ancient animal from the fossilized contents of its stomach. Plesiosaurs – sea-dwelling reptiles from the time of the dinosaurs – ate fish and ammonites. We know this partly from the evidence provided by the teeth – but fossils of their last meals can also be found within their skeletons. In the case of one plesiosaur skeleton, the flow of water through the rock where it lay replaced the food material in its stomach with the mineral silica. The result was a glittering "food fossil" made of opal.

Mummified skin – but most of the skin covering has not been preserved

Edmontosaurus was a duck-billed dinosaur

MUMMIFICATION

Spectacular finds of *Edmontosaurus* from Alberta, Canada, have preserved impressions of the skin around parts of the body, including the head, shoulder, and hand. These "mummified" fossils show that the skin was made up of rounded scales, and that it was deeply wrinkled in the shoulder area. The remains of some padding behind the hooves, to help the feet bear the animal's weight, have also been found.

A palaeontologist from the University of Chicago, USA

Paul Sereno on the site of a dig in Africa

BIG GAME HUNTERS

Modern dinosaur hunters use much more advanced techniques than those of the 19th century. Today's experts make minute examinations of the surrounding rocks and environment, as well as carefully collecting the bones. Paul Sereno of Chicago, USA, is one of the most successful of modern dinosaur hunters, having excavated dozens of new specimens in North Africa.

THEIR WORLD

TWO MURDEROUS *ALLOSAURUS* STALK a herd of peaceful *Camarasaurus* through a riverside forest. A young, inexperienced *Camarasaurus* ventures alone into the open, where it is vulnerable. The predators attack, leaping and ripping at it with teeth and claws until their massive target is brought down. Then, they settle down to feast. In fact, we do not know for certain how *Allosaurus* hunted and fed – whether singly, as a pack, or even as scavengers – but this is an acceptable theory.

EXPLORING AN *ALLOSAURUS* ATTACK

1 **Hunting ground:** *the forest along a dried-up stream is home to hunting theropods and their sauropod prey*

2 **The predators:** *a pair of Allosaurus work together to separate an individual sauropod from its herd*

3 **The prey:** *a large Camarasaurus is safe as long as it does not stray from the herd*

4 **The weapons:** *an Allosaurus uses both its teeth and its claws to attack, injure, and exhaust its prey*

5 **The killer:** *the more agile of the Allosaurus pair leaps on to the tired Camarasaurus and kills it*

6 **The scavengers:** *pterosaurs and other small creatures gather around, awaiting any left-overs*

7 **The sentry:** *the stronger Allosaurus stands guard against other big meat-eaters intent on stealing their kill*

8 **Food:** *the flesh and internal organs of this large sauropod could nourish these theropods for a long time*

9 **Remains:** *the left-over bones will be washed away in the next flood, and possibly fossilized for eternity*

Tyrannosaurus was one of the largest predatory dinosaurs

A FEROCIOUS ARGUMENT

Some dinosaurs probably fought with others of their own kind, as well as with those of different species. A *Tyrannosaurus* would have been fiercely protective of any meaty kill or find that it had made. To ensure its own well-being, it would have defended such a catch against any other *Tyrannosaurus* that attempted to take a share.

CONFLICT

ALL DINOSAURS FACED THE DAILY challenge of how to survive. Both plant-eating and meat-eating dinosaurs developed a variety of strategies to help them find food and avoid attack from predators. The big plant-eating dinosaurs that thrived in the lush forests of the Jurassic period were a potentially huge food resource for others. It is no surprise, then, that large meat-eating dinosaurs evolved to feed on them. But the danger posed by these predators also led to the evolution of formidable defensive measures that the hunters had to face. Fierce competition for prey also led predators to develop increasingly deadly weapons. As a result, a frightening range of dinosaur claws, teeth, and armour was on display during the Mesozoic.

The very small forelimbs show that Tyrannosaurus probably got most of its food by scavenging

The horny claw would have been even longer than this – half as long again as the bony support shown here

Finger bone

Razor-like spines made Gastonia a fearsome sight

THE KILLING CLAW

Claws were the main killing weapons of meat-eating theropod ("beast feet") dinosaurs. The forelimbs of *Allosaurus* were made up of heavily-muscled arms ending in three-fingered, grasping hands that had enormous claws. One finger was bigger and stronger than the others, but they all had huge, hooked claws. Such hands were used to hold the prey down firmly while the theropod ripped off its flesh.

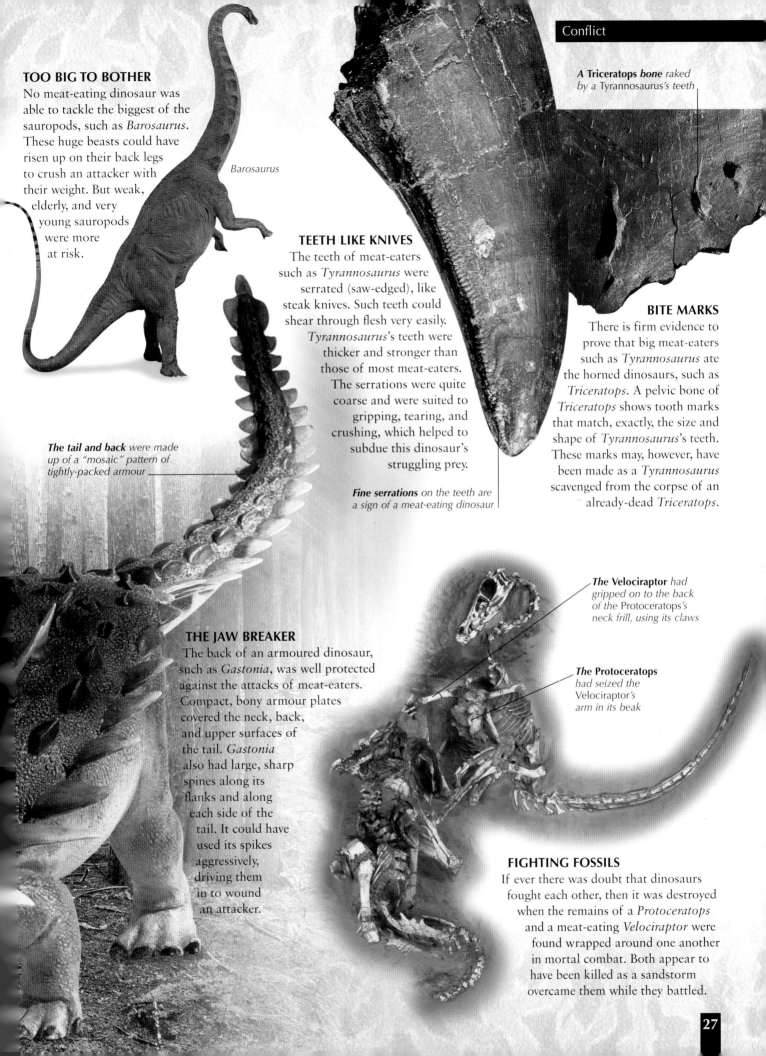

A Triceratops bone raked by a Tyrannosaurus's teeth

TOO BIG TO BOTHER

No meat-eating dinosaur was able to tackle the biggest of the sauropods, such as *Barosaurus*. These huge beasts could have risen up on their back legs to crush an attacker with their weight. But weak, elderly, and very young sauropods were more at risk.

Barosaurus

TEETH LIKE KNIVES

The teeth of meat-eaters such as *Tyrannosaurus* were serrated (saw-edged), like steak knives. Such teeth could shear through flesh very easily. *Tyrannosaurus*'s teeth were thicker and stronger than those of most meat-eaters. The serrations were quite coarse and were suited to gripping, tearing, and crushing, which helped to subdue this dinosaur's struggling prey.

Fine serrations on the teeth are a sign of a meat-eating dinosaur

BITE MARKS

There is firm evidence to prove that big meat-eaters such as *Tyrannosaurus* ate the horned dinosaurs, such as *Triceratops*. A pelvic bone of *Triceratops* shows tooth marks that match, exactly, the size and shape of *Tyrannosaurus*'s teeth. These marks may, however, have been made as a *Tyrannosaurus* scavenged from the corpse of an already-dead *Triceratops*.

The tail and back were made up of a "mosaic" pattern of tightly-packed armour

THE JAW BREAKER

The back of an armoured dinosaur, such as *Gastonia*, was well protected against the attacks of meat-eaters. Compact, bony armour plates covered the neck, back, and upper surfaces of the tail. *Gastonia* also had large, sharp spines along its flanks and along each side of the tail. It could have used its spikes aggressively, driving them in to wound an attacker.

The Velociraptor had gripped on to the back of the Protoceratops's neck frill, using its claws

The Protoceratops had seized the Velociraptor's arm in its beak

FIGHTING FOSSILS

If ever there was doubt that dinosaurs fought each other, then it was destroyed when the remains of a *Protoceratops* and a meat-eating *Velociraptor* were found wrapped around one another in mortal combat. Both appear to have been killed as a sandstorm overcame them while they battled.

ACHES AND PAINS
Some natural repair where this *Iguanodon* hip bone once broke shows that the animal suffered an injury but survived. The bone knitted itself together slightly out of line – so it may not have been as good as new, but at least it allowed the animal to live another day.

— Point of fracture

DINOSAUR DUNG
Animal droppings are sometimes preserved, as a fossil called a coprolite. Coprolites may contain bone fragments or mineralized vegetable material, which can tell us a lot about the diet of an extinct animal such as a dinosaur.

FOSSIL STORIES

THE FOSSILIZED BONES OF A DINOSAUR do not just tell us what the dinosaur might have looked like. They can reveal all sorts of things about the health and lifestyle of the animal. Fossils and sediments found at the excavation site teach scientists about a dinosaur's ecology – its relationship with its environment and the other animals and plants that lived there. Experts can tell the difference between damage done to a bone after death (a study known as taphonomy) and damage suffered during life (a study known as pathology). Pathological studies have revealed some fascinating stories about the various accidents and diseases that affected dinosaurs while they were still alive.

A bone cancer cell, shown greatly enlarged

NASTY DISEASES
Many diseases can leave their mark on the bones of an animal. A swelling – such as this one on the tail bone of a duck-billed hadrosaur – is a sign that the animal suffered from cancer while it was alive. The cancer led to tumours growing throughout the body.

Tumour on the bone – bone cancer leads to this type of swelling

BAD BONES
Fossilized dinosaur bones can show the wear and tear of everyday life. The foot bones of a heavy *Iguanodon* show that it had a condition called arthritis, which caused a frilly growth of bone between the toe joints. The disease probably developed during old age, after a lifetime of pressure on the hind limbs.

These toe bones have fused (joined) together

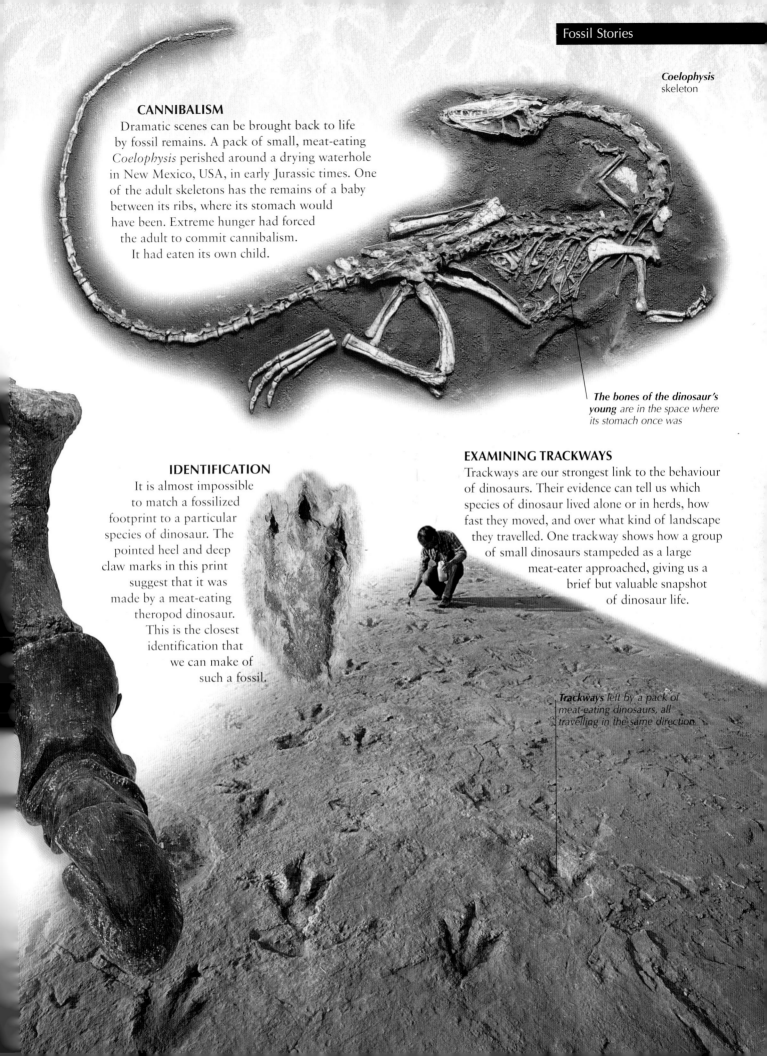

Coelophysis
skeleton

CANNIBALISM

Dramatic scenes can be brought back to life
by fossil remains. A pack of small, meat-eating
Coelophysis perished around a drying waterhole
in New Mexico, USA, in early Jurassic times. One
of the adult skeletons has the remains of a baby
between its ribs, where its stomach would
have been. Extreme hunger had forced
the adult to commit cannibalism.
It had eaten its own child.

**The bones of the dinosaur's
young** are in the space where
its stomach once was

IDENTIFICATION

It is almost impossible
to match a fossilized
footprint to a particular
species of dinosaur. The
pointed heel and deep
claw marks in this print
suggest that it was
made by a meat-eating
theropod dinosaur.
This is the closest
identification that
we can make of
such a fossil.

EXAMINING TRACKWAYS

Trackways are our strongest link to the behaviour
of dinosaurs. Their evidence can tell us which
species of dinosaur lived alone or in herds, how
fast they moved, and over what kind of landscape
they travelled. One trackway shows how a group
of small dinosaurs stampeded as a large
meat-eater approached, giving us a
brief but valuable snapshot
of dinosaur life.

Trackways left by a pack of
meat-eating dinosaurs, all
travelling in the same direction

CHANGING FACES

The head and neck of Apatosaurus, with the correct skull in place

W HAT DID A DINOSAUR ACTUALLY look like? How did it live? What colour was it? These are questions that have dogged the study of palaeontology for centuries. Today, a wider range of knowledge brings us closer to the answers – but that knowledge has taken a long time to gather. In the past, palaeontologists had to rely on much smaller scraps of evidence, and their theories could change from one day to the next as new fossils were unearthed. As each day goes by, such experts find out a little more to change our ideas about dinosaurs.

SHAPE-SHIFTING

When the scattered remains of *Iguanodon* were discovered in the 1820s, palaeontologists first imagined the dinosaur as a kind of giant, four-footed lizard. Complete skeletons found in Belgium, in the 1880s, then suggested that *Iguanodon* walked on its hind legs like a kangaroo. Today's scientists believe that this creature was indeed four-footed, but that it could walk on its hind legs some of the time.

Kangaroo-posed Iguanodon – *the early 20th-century restoration*

Semi-quadrupedal (four-footed) Iguanodon – *the late 20th-century restoration*

Water-dwelling Corythosaurus, *which experts no longer accept as being correct*

Land-based Corythosaurus

LAND OR WATER?

Early ideas about the duck-billed dinosaurs, such as *Corythosaurus*, suggested that they could swim. The front feet seemed to be webbed, and the tail was flattened like a crocodile's. They also had a duck-like head. But later studies showed that the "webbing" on the fingers was a weight-bearing pad, and that the tail could not have supported swimming muscles.

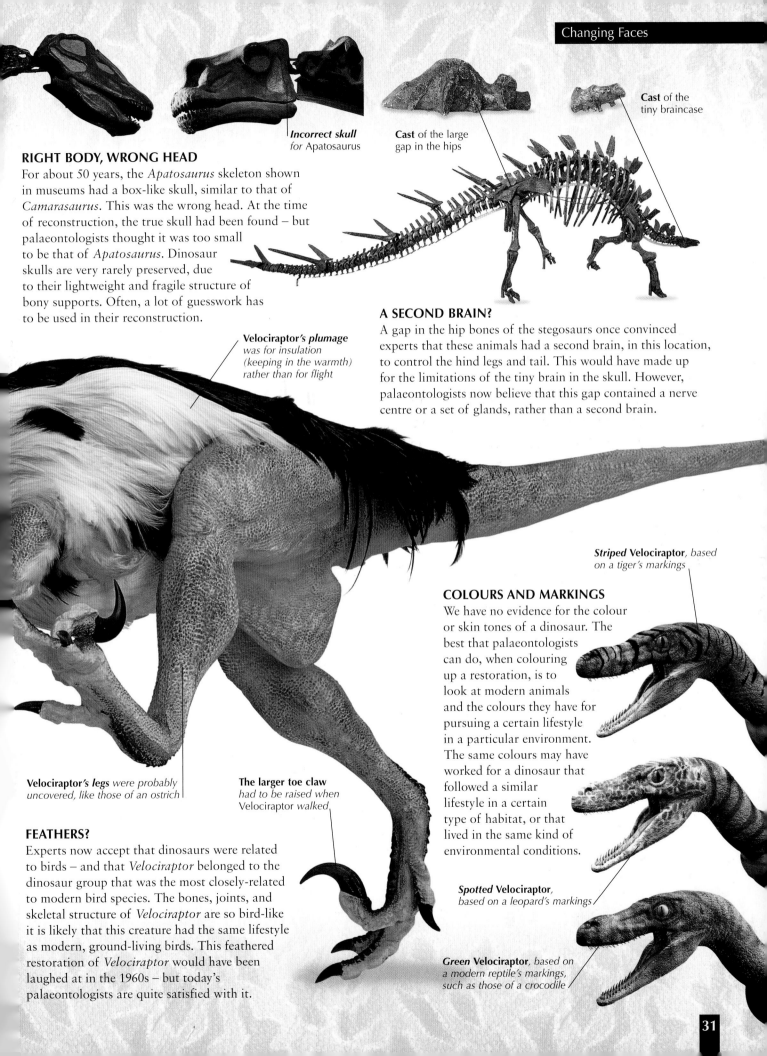

Incorrect skull
for Apatosaurus

Cast of the large
gap in the hips

Cast of the
tiny braincase

RIGHT BODY, WRONG HEAD

For about 50 years, the *Apatosaurus* skeleton shown
in museums had a box-like skull, similar to that of
Camarasaurus. This was the wrong head. At the time
of reconstruction, the true skull had been found – but
palaeontologists thought it was too small
to be that of *Apatosaurus*. Dinosaur
skulls are very rarely preserved, due
to their lightweight and fragile structure of
bony supports. Often, a lot of guesswork has
to be used in their reconstruction.

Velociraptor's plumage
was for insulation
(keeping in the warmth)
rather than for flight

A SECOND BRAIN?

A gap in the hip bones of the stegosaurs once convinced
experts that these animals had a second brain, in this location,
to control the hind legs and tail. This would have made up
for the limitations of the tiny brain in the skull. However,
palaeontologists now believe that this gap contained a nerve
centre or a set of glands, rather than a second brain.

Striped Velociraptor, based
on a tiger's markings

COLOURS AND MARKINGS

We have no evidence for the colour
or skin tones of a dinosaur. The
best that palaeontologists
can do, when colouring
up a restoration, is to
look at modern animals
and the colours they have for
pursuing a certain lifestyle
in a particular environment.
The same colours may have
worked for a dinosaur that
followed a similar
lifestyle in a certain
type of habitat, or that
lived in the same kind of
environmental conditions.

Velociraptor's legs were probably
uncovered, like those of an ostrich

The larger toe claw
had to be raised when
Velociraptor *walked*

FEATHERS?

Experts now accept that dinosaurs were related
to birds – and that *Velociraptor* belonged to the
dinosaur group that was the most closely-related
to modern bird species. The bones, joints, and
skeletal structure of *Velociraptor* are so bird-like
it is likely that this creature had the same lifestyle
as modern, ground-living birds. This feathered
restoration of *Velociraptor* would have been
laughed at in the 1960s – but today's
palaeontologists are quite satisfied with it.

Spotted Velociraptor,
based on a leopard's markings

Green Velociraptor, based on
a modern reptile's markings,
such as those of a crocodile

UP CLOSE

IT IS NO LONGER POSSIBLE for us to get this close to an animal like the horned *Styracosaurus*. Nor would this have been a very safe thing to do! But if we could, we would see how well designed this animal was. The bony frill around its neck supported the jaw muscles and protected the shoulders from a head-on attack – but it was also there for display. Its massive area, along with the horny ornament, made the animal look much bigger and more aggressive than it actually was. The patterns and colouration were also important, such as the large "eye" markings that would have struck fear into any animal that it faced.

FRILL FEATURES

The ceratopsians – plant-eating dinosaurs with beaks and a bony frill – all had the same body plan. The only variations were in the heads of the different species. Some had a single horn, some three or more, some had horns on the frill, and others had none at all. These various ornaments helped to set apart one herd of ceratopsians from another on the plains of the late Cretaceous.

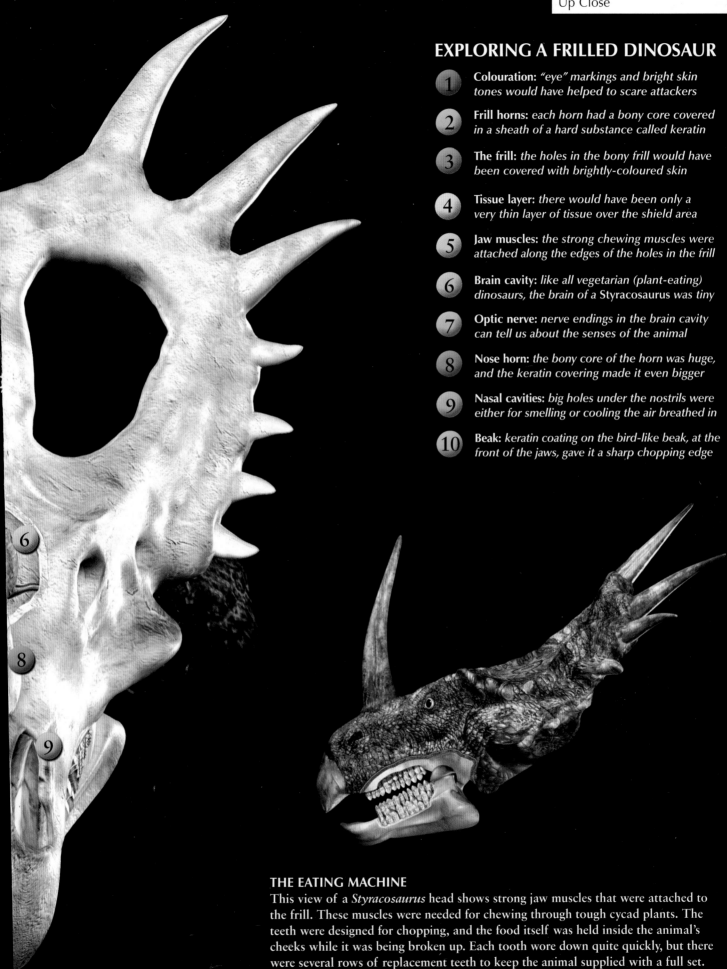

EXPLORING A FRILLED DINOSAUR

1 **Colouration:** *"eye" markings and bright skin tones would have helped to scare attackers*

2 **Frill horns:** *each horn had a bony core covered in a sheath of a hard substance called keratin*

3 **The frill:** *the holes in the bony frill would have been covered with brightly-coloured skin*

4 **Tissue layer:** *there would have been only a very thin layer of tissue over the shield area*

5 **Jaw muscles:** *the strong chewing muscles were attached along the edges of the holes in the frill*

6 **Brain cavity:** *like all vegetarian (plant-eating) dinosaurs, the brain of a Styracosaurus was tiny*

7 **Optic nerve:** *nerve endings in the brain cavity can tell us about the senses of the animal*

8 **Nose horn:** *the bony core of the horn was huge, and the keratin covering made it even bigger*

9 **Nasal cavities:** *big holes under the nostrils were either for smelling or cooling the air breathed in*

10 **Beak:** *keratin coating on the bird-like beak, at the front of the jaws, gave it a sharp chopping edge*

THE EATING MACHINE

This view of a *Styracosaurus* head shows strong jaw muscles that were attached to the frill. These muscles were needed for chewing through tough cycad plants. The teeth were designed for chopping, and the food itself was held inside the animal's cheeks while it was being broken up. Each tooth wore down quite quickly, but there were several rows of replacement teeth to keep the animal supplied with a full set.

33

MICRORAPTOR

This strange entry into the list of half-bird, half-dinosaur creatures was unearthed in China. It is called *Microraptor*. A fossil of this small, meat-eating dinosaur shows that it had a full set of feathers on its body, and flight feathers on its hind legs. According to experts, this little dinosaur-bird could spread out all of its limbs to form a gliding "plane" shape – similar to that of a modern flying squirrel – so that it could sail from tree to tree.

Microraptor *had flying feathers on its arms and legs*

Meat-eating *dinosaur jaws*

Deinonychus

MISSING LINKS

HERE IS A COMMON QUESTION – what are the closest living relatives of the dinosaurs? The answer is – the birds. About 50 years ago, this idea would have horrified people. At that time, the most popular image of a dinosaur was that of a lumbering, cold-blooded monster. The notion of birds being related to dinosaurs had been around since the discovery of *Archaeopteryx* in the 1860s, but it was not until the fossil finds of agile, bird-like dinosaurs – such as *Deinonychus*, found 100 years later – that the idea truly took hold. Today, most palaeontologists accept this link, which has been strengthened by the recent discoveries, in China, of many different Mesozoic animals that had a fascinating mixture of dinosaur and bird features.

Joints in the wrists *like those in a bird's wing*

Curved claws

Archaeopteryx

The skeleton *of Archaeopteryx was that of a dinosaur*

The feathers and wings *were those of a bird*

DINO-BIRDS

At the height of 19th-century dinosaur study, one of the most famous discoveries was a fossil of *Archaeopteryx*, excavated from very fine Jurassic limestone deposits in Germany. Palaeontologists first identified the fossil as that of a bird because of the impression of wings and feathers preserved in the soft rock. However, the fossil also showed fingers on the wings, a long bony tail, and toothy jaws rather than teeth. It appeared to be a perfect mixture of dinosaur and bird.

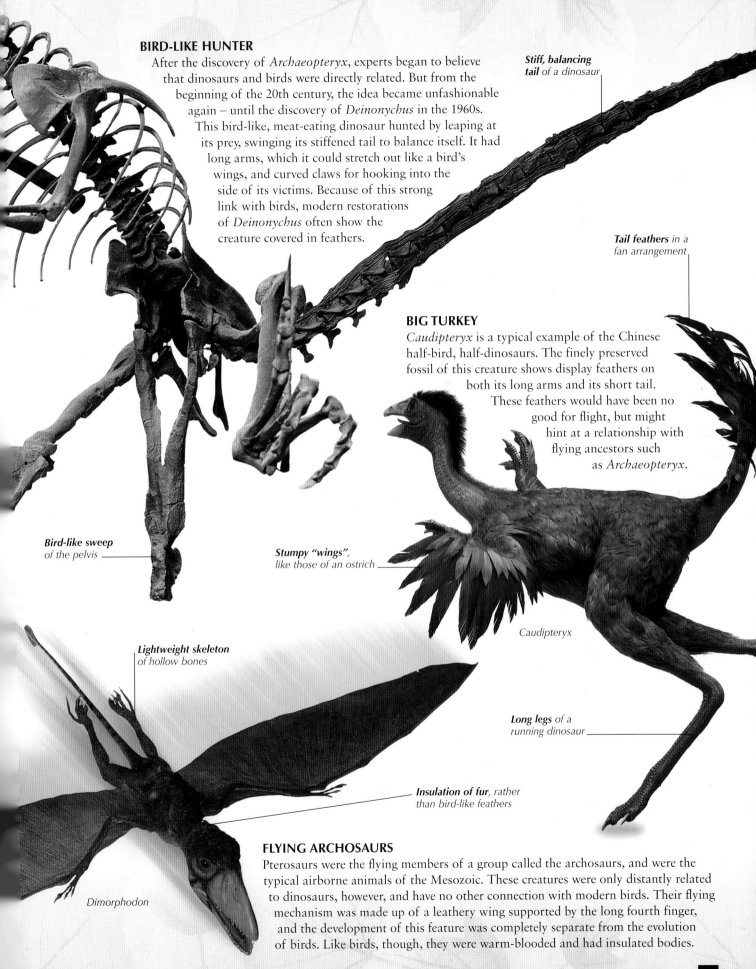

BIRD-LIKE HUNTER

After the discovery of *Archaeopteryx*, experts began to believe that dinosaurs and birds were directly related. But from the beginning of the 20th century, the idea became unfashionable again – until the discovery of *Deinonychus* in the 1960s. This bird-like, meat-eating dinosaur hunted by leaping at its prey, swinging its stiffened tail to balance itself. It had long arms, which it could stretch out like a bird's wings, and curved claws for hooking into the side of its victims. Because of this strong link with birds, modern restorations of *Deinonychus* often show the creature covered in feathers.

Stiff, balancing tail of a dinosaur

Tail feathers in a fan arrangement

BIG TURKEY

Caudipteryx is a typical example of the Chinese half-bird, half-dinosaurs. The finely preserved fossil of this creature shows display feathers on both its long arms and its short tail. These feathers would have been no good for flight, but might hint at a relationship with flying ancestors such as *Archaeopteryx*.

Bird-like sweep of the pelvis

Stumpy "wings", like those of an ostrich

Caudipteryx

Lightweight skeleton of hollow bones

Long legs of a running dinosaur

Insulation of fur, rather than bird-like feathers

Dimorphodon

FLYING ARCHOSAURS

Pterosaurs were the flying members of a group called the archosaurs, and were the typical airborne animals of the Mesozoic. These creatures were only distantly related to dinosaurs, however, and have no other connection with modern birds. Their flying mechanism was made up of a leathery wing supported by the long fourth finger, and the development of this feature was completely separate from the evolution of birds. Like birds, though, they were warm-blooded and had insulated bodies.

VOLCANIC ACTIVITY
Half of the Indian sub-continent is built up of lava flows that erupted about 65 million years ago. The amount of climatic change produced by these eruptions must have had an effect on the ecosystems around at that time, possibly wiping out many species.

DYING OUT

METEOR IMPACT
The best explanation for the dinosaurs' extinction is that a comet or giant meteor collided with the Earth about 65 million years ago. Impact craters on moons and planets show that this occurs fairly regularly in our Solar System. In fact, the evidence of impact craters on our planet proves that such events have happened repeatedly throughout the Earth's history.

Fossil of **Lepidotes** *– a Mesozoic heavy-fish*

THE AGE OF THE DINOSAURS came to an end suddenly. But "suddenly", to a geologist, could mean a few days or as much as half a million years. Most experts believe that a comet or meteorite struck the Earth, millions of years ago, and caused so much environmental damage that it wiped out about 70 per cent of the Earth's animal life. However, there is evidence that other things were happening at that time, such as volcanic eruptions and changes in climate. Fossil records suggest that, at the end of the Cretaceous period, there were far fewer species of dinosaur in existence than earlier in the Mesozoic Era. It is possible that the dinosaurs were dying out at this time, and that an impact from space simply delivered the final blow.

HOW FOSSILS FORM
Fossils left behind in the ground tell us about species that have been made extinct (wiped out). A fossil can be the original hard part of an animal; the cast (impression) of original material that has dissolved away; a "petrification", where the original material is replaced by minerals; or even the footprint or burrow of an animal. Diagenesis is the name for the process by which sediments become rock and organisms become fossils.

RADIATION

Life on Earth is always at risk from cosmic rays. The Earth's magnetic field shields the planet from their harmful effects – but every now and again, this field collapses and reverses. This magnetic reversal could result in mass extinctions if it happened at the same time as an outburst of rays from some activity in space, such as the supernova of an exploding star.

VIRUS ALERT

Towards the end of the Cretaceous, many of the world's isolated landmasses joined up, allowing animals to spread into new areas. Migrating animals could easily have spread diseases among the native animals of another region – diseases to which they, themselves, had become immune. This could have resulted in widespread epidemics among the various populations of dinosaurs, which may have led to their extinction.

CLIMATE CHANGE

The Earth's climate is constantly changing, and it became cooler at the end of the Cretaceous period. This followed a long spell of stable (unchanging) conditions, which may have reduced the ability of the dinosaurs to adapt to environmental changes. In later years, the changing conditions of the Cretaceous may have caused them to die out.

THE STUDY OF DEATH

Along with the study of diagenesis – of how fossils form – goes the study of taphonomy. Taphonomy is all about what happens to an animal between the time of its death and the time of its fossilization. The twisted position of this *Baryonyx* shows that it lay exposed and shrivelled up, for some time, before being buried in the ground.

IT CAME FROM SPACE...

Perhaps the strongest evidence of an impact from space lies in the rocks of the Yucatan peninsula, in Mexico. The sub-surface rock structures show a circular formation, known as the Chicxulub structure, tens of kilometres in diameter. Scientists think this is the remains of an impact crater from the end of the Cretaceous. At the time, the impact crater would have formed circular rings of mountains, like those in this picture.

INDEX

ACKNOWLEDGEMENTS

**Dorling Kindersley would
like to thank:**
Dorothy Frame for the index, Alyson
Lacewing for proof reading, and
Sarah Mills for DK Picture
Library research.

**The publisher would like to
thank the following for their kind
permission to reproduce their
photographs:**
Key: a = above; b = below;
c = centre; l = left; r = right;
t = top; ace = acetate

alamy.com: Royal Geographical
Society 10tl; **American Museum**
of Natural History: 3bl, 6bl, 10bl,
27br; **Canadian Museum of
Nature, Ottawa, Canada:** photo by
R. Martin 32-33 (back of acetate
sheet); **Carnegie Museum:** 30t;
Corbis: 15 bckgrd; Tom Bean 29b;
Dutheil Didier 23br; Layne Kennedy
20tl; Gail Mooney 14c; Richard T.
Nowitz 18bl, 19b; Michael T.
Sedam 26b bckgrd; Sygma / Close
Murray 21b; Underwood and
Underwood 19tr; Michael S.
Yamashita 26bl; **Dinosaur State
Park:** endpapers; **Christine M.
Douglas:** 14-15; © **The Field
Museum:** # GN89087_24c 14bl;
Chris Brochu GEO 86195_3c 20tr;

Boban Filipovic: 34tl; **Getty
Images:** Harald Sund 3br, 10-11,
12-13, 14-15, 30bc; **Jonathan
Hateley:** 15bl; **Dave Martill /
University of Portsmouth:** 23tr;
Museum of the Rockies: 8bl, 8-9
(back of acetate sheet, bl) 11bl,
27tr; **The Natural History Museum,
London:** 10tr, 14cl, 21tl, 28-29, 29t;
**North Carolina Museum of Natural
Sciences:** 22bl; **Oxford University
Museum:** 18tr; **Luis Rey:** 30-31;
Royal Saskatchewan Museum: 28tr;
**Royal Tyrrell Museum of
Paleontology:** 12tc,13bl, 19cl,
22-23; **Science Photo Library:**
Chris Butler 3cl, 7cr, 23cr; Tony
Craddock 37cr; Martin Dohrn /
Stephen Winkworth 6tl; Mehau
Kulyk 36tl, 37tl; S. R. Maglione 3tr,

15b bckgrd, 18-19, 20-21, 22-23;
Peter Menzel 23ca; Larry Miller
29c; NIBSC 37tr; Alfred Pasieka
28cl; D. Van Ravenswaay 36-37;
Soames Summerhays 36tr;
Senekenberg Nature Museum: 20bl;
David Varrichio: Museum of the
Rockies 8br; **Yale University
Peabody Museum Of Natural
History:** 31tcl, 35t.

All other images
© Dorling Kindersley.
**For further imformation,
see: www.dkimages.com**

Every effort has been made
to trace copyright holders of
photographs. The publishers
apologize for any omissions.